D0874080

In and Out
with Dick and Jane

In and Out
with Dick and Jane

A Loving Parody

Ross MacDonald and James Victore

Abrams Image
New York

This book is a parody and has not been prepared, approved, or authorized by the creators of the "Dick and Jane" reading primers for children.

Dick and Jane® is a registered trademark of Pearson Education, Inc.

Library of Congress Cataloging-in-Publication Data

MacDonald, Ross, 1957-
In and out with Dick and Jane : a loving parody / Ross MacDonald and James Victore.
p. cm.
ISBN 978-0-8109-9759-2 (alk. paper)
1. Readers (Primary)--Humor. 2. American wit and humor. 3. Children's stories, American--Parodies, imitations, etc. I. Victore, James, 1962- II. Title.
PN6231.R36M33 2011
818'.602--dc22

2010037662

Text copyright © 2011 Ross MacDonald and James Victore
Illustrations copyright © 2011 Ross MacDonald

Printed and bound in China
10 9 8 7 6 5 4 3 2 1

Abrams Image books are available at special discounts when purchased in quantity for premiums and promotions as well as fundraising or educational use. Special editions can also be created to specification. For details, contact specialmarkets@abramsbooks.com or the address below.

THE ART OF BOOKS SINCE 1949
115 West 18th Street
New York, NY 10011
www.abramsbooks.com

Contents

Our Neighborhood

This is our neighborhood.
Lots of nice people live here.

These are the Joneses.
Mrs. Jones is pretty.

This is Mr. Jeffrey.

He plays a clown at parties.

He's good at tying things.

The Whites are scientists.
They let us see their secret
laboratory.

Everyone in the neighborhood is different . . .

. . . but not too different.

Good neighbors help each other. Once, sometimes twice, a month, we help Mr. Franco clean out his garage.

We are such good helpers.

Our Town

There is a lot to do in our town.
We go to church.
We learn about morals and
values and angels.

The priest there helps guide the little children.

At the other end of town there
is a bookstore and a shoe store
and a toy store.

But we go to the big, big, BIG
store. They have everything.

Mother buys lots and lots of things, but it doesn't cost her anything . . .

EASY-CHARGE

21 08 9760   45514 2

MRS SCOT FOR MAN

. . . because she has this!

A Day at School

In school, we learn many things. We learn math and we learn to read. We learn that we are all different . . . especially the boys and the girls.

We learn to be good citizens.

NO:

- TOUCHING
- TALKING
- BACK TALKING
- ROUGH HOUSING
- BULLYING
- PLAYING
- PRAYING
- OVERT ETHNICITY
- OVERT RELIGIOUS SYMBOLS
- DISCRIMINATION ON THE BASIS OF ETHNICITY OR RELIGION
- PEANUTS

Billy has a hard time at school.

He can't sit still.

He can't pay attention.

Now Billy can concentrate.

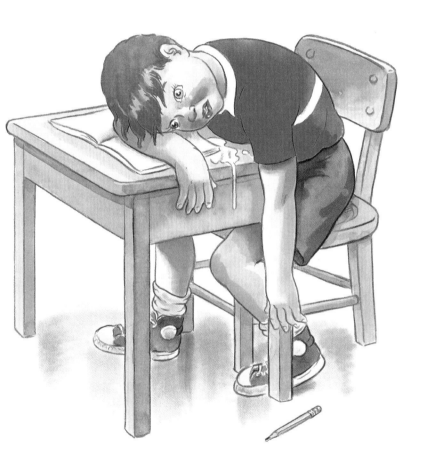

Lunchtime is our favorite.

School has the best lunches.

Learning is fun.

After School

At school, we worked hard.
Now the bell rings and school
is over.

After school, some kids play
sports.

Some have hobbies.

And some are in youth clubs.

But Billy is a latchkey kid.
He has his own house key.
His house is full of things—fun
things—his mommy's things.
Let's play at Billy's house.

Be quiet. Billy's mom is sleeping.

She smells funny.

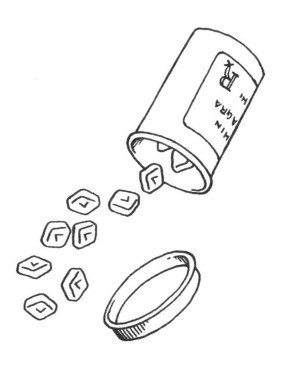

At Billy's house,
we play many things.
We play doctor.

We play fireman.

We play dress up.

Billy likes dress up.

A Day at the Fair

The fair is in town!
There are lots of people
at the fair.

Oh, Sally, see the pretty flags,
see the rides, see the balloons!

Let's visit the animal barn.
See the cute animals.
See the cute ponies and the
cute lambs and the cute pigs.
Sally wants to pet the piglets.

Cotton candy

Yummy drinks

Meat

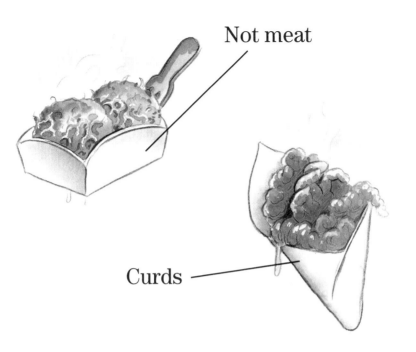

Not meat

Curds

Daddy loves the food at the fair.

Big-n-Cheezy
nachos

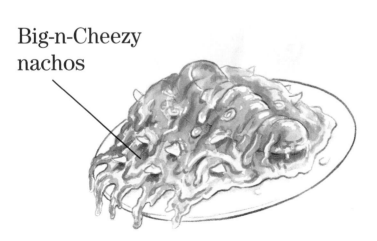

Time for the rides.
Daddy asks the carny lots
of questions about the
bolts and the bare wires
and the duct tape.

We go round and round.

We go up, up, up.

We go down, down, down.

Over and over again.

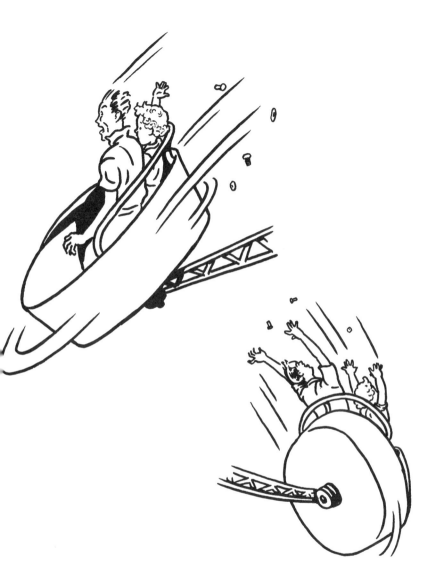

The carny gives Daddy an
extra long ride.

Cotton candy

Yummy drinks

Meat

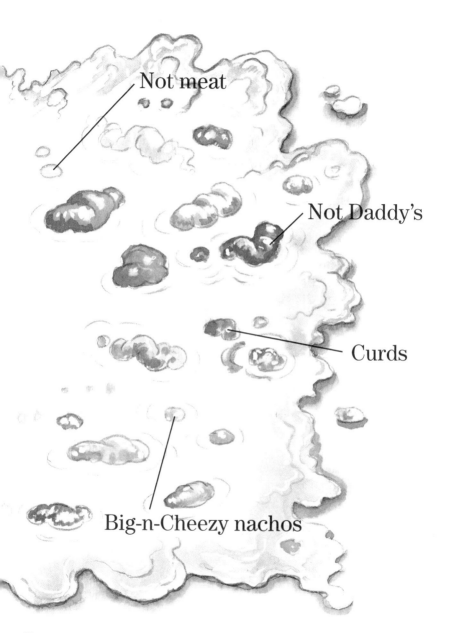

Not meat

Not Daddy's

Curds

Big-n-Cheezy nachos

See all the pretty colors.

A Visit to the Country

Let's take a trip to the country.
Nature is so beautiful.

We feed the ducks.

We help nature by picking up trash.

Sally, NO!

Saving the outdoors is important.

DONATIONS

HELP KEEP
OUR PARK
BEAUTIFUL

It's fun to visit nature.

Ross MacDonald is a contributing artist for *Vanity Fair*. His award-winning illustrations have appeared in the *New Yorker*, the *Atlantic*, the *Wall Street Journal*, and *Rolling Stone*. He was also the subject of a one-man retrospective at the *New York Times*.

James Victore is an independent graphic designer based in New York City whose clients include Moët & Chandon, Target, Amnesty International, the Shakespeare Project, the *New York Times*, and MTV. He has won an Emmy for television animation, and gold and silver medals from the New York Art Directors Club.